D1112365

If found, please return this journal to:

....

Everything
Beautiful
in Its Time

A FAMILY JOURNAL

Also by Jenna Bush Hager

Everything Beautiful in Its Time

Our Great Big Backyard
  (with Laura Bush)

Read All About It!
  (with Laura Bush)

Ana's Story: A Journey of Hope

Sisters First: Stories from Our
  Wild and Wonderful Life
  (with Barbara Pierce Bush)

Jenna Bush Hager

Everything Beautiful in Its Time

A FAMILY JOURNAL

MORROW
GIFT

To those who taught me to write:

MY PRECIOUS GRANDPARENTS

WHO WANTED TO MAKE SURE

WE NEVER TOOK A MOMENT

FOR GRANTED

Write it all down so you never forget!

Contents

A Letter from
Me to You

My paternal grandmother, Barbara, whom we called Ganny, woke every morning before the sun was up to write about her life. Often what she committed to the pages of her journals were musings (and grievances!) about her grandchildren, her friends, or her beloved husband. As she grew older, her handwriting became labored, her sentences shorter, and so she reluctantly began to type her daily observations instead.

Once when I was visiting her in Maine, I used her office to print something for my work on the *Today* show. When I opened the computer, her journal popped up. I glanced at it: *The twins are here. What fun they are!* I quickly shut the file, not wanting to invade her privacy, but I was touched to

discover that she had taken the time to mention me. Now, decades later, I think, *Of course she did.* Her family was her biggest inspiration and her truest love. Writing about us was her way to cherish our time together.

Her husband, the former president George H. W. Bush, whom we called Gampy, also kept a journal. He wrote about affairs of state and about his hopes and fears for our nation, but he also wrote about his family, and particularly about his wife. After Ganny passed away, my Aunt Doro found a note in one of his journals. It read: *Please read this at Bar's funeral*:

And when she shall die

Take her and cut her out in the stars,

And she will make the face of heaven so fine

That all the world will be in love with night

And pay no worship to the garish sun.

These are lines from *Romeo and Juliet*, which seemed appropriate to us because we always thought of our grandparents' love as Shakespearean.

As I read those words and the pages around them, I realized that my grandparents' journals and the letters they wrote me were the greatest gifts they could have given. These poignant reminders of fishing in the ocean, opening presents beneath the Christmas tree, attending cousins' weddings, and recovering from illnesses—they almost leap off the page and play themselves for me like home movies.

And now I am the one who is keeping a journal about my family. After losing three of my grandparents in the span of a year, I found myself comforted by waking early to write down my feelings and memories. It was as if by writing down everything and recalling cherished details about my relatives who had passed, I could keep them close. Grief hits hard, and in waves. But grief is the sign of true love; we grieve something only when we love it deeply enough to miss it.

As I wrote these reminiscences about my grandparents, I found myself talking to them—telling them about me and my sister and my children, whom they loved so much. As I took note in this journal of my children's first steps, first words—and, yes, even their first temper tantrums!—I found myself paying closer attention to each precious moment of their young lives, and feeling more deeply the joys and sorrows of life. This is something I learned from Gampy. Here is something he wrote in his journal near the end of his life: "I used to seek broad horizons in life and found plenty. Now I don't care if I can't even see Ogunquit. Limited horizons are okay by me just so long as family's in view."

As I cherish my grandparents' journals, so I hope my children will be grateful for mine. If nothing else, by reading in these pages the stories of their parents and grandparents they will know where they came from and they will know how very deeply they were loved. My baby Hal was born within a year of his three great-grandparents' death. It breaks my heart to know that he will never know them, and yet through their words about our family and through mine, perhaps in another way he will come to know them.

Readers of my book *Everything Beautiful in Its Time,* about my year of love and loss, have told me that the book inspired them to tell their own family stories, which I consider the highest honor. Those messages inspired me to put together this keepsake journal, full of selections from the book and related questions. I hope these prompts will help you reminiscence and pay tribute to your loved ones.

Please make this book your own! I've tried to keep the

questions general; not every question will apply to every one of you. Families take many different forms. For example, some people have never met one or more of their grandparents or parents. Others have big, close families full of parents, step-parents, aunts, uncles, in-laws, ex–in-laws, and third cousins once removed. Whatever our circumstances, our family tree is part of what makes us who we are, and it's important to document.

Get as creative as you'd like. If you don't have your own children, perhaps in those spaces you'd like to write about your favorite niece or about the role children have played or not played in your life. If you're an only child, you could write about a close friend or cousin who was like a brother or sister. If you can't remember your grandparents, perhaps you'd like to dream about who they might have been. What's important is that you identify what *you* find valuable in your family's story and write it down for yourself and for those who follow.

You will notice that I encourage you to write a number of letters in this journal—to a grandparent, parent, child, teacher, friend. Please consider copying out these letters and sending them to any one of the recipients who are still around. Letters are one of the best ways to tell people about their significance to us. Heartfelt letters can transform the sender and the receiver. But even if we never send these letters, they can help us honor our relatives and heroes.

As the saying goes, the years are short and the days are long. It's easy to get caught up in daily living and forget that our loved ones won't always be here to influence our lives. I hope as you write in these pages you feel free to grieve and to love, and that reading back over your words and stories brings you and your family inspiration, comfort, and connection for many years to come!

Love,
Jenna

PART I

Your Family Tree

All About You

What is your name?

....

What is your birthdate?

....

How old are you?

....

Where were you born?

....

Where did you grow up?

....

Where are you living now?

....

"There are traits we

pass on to those we love.

Yes, genetic gifts:

eye color, birthmarks, dimples.

But we also share a more

ineffable inheritance:

our stories, histories,

and traditions."

Your Letter to the Future

Imagine one of your descendants
coming upon this journal years in the future.
Write them a letter about the year in which you're
writing these words. What is happening in the world,
in your country, in your family?

....

....

....

....

....

....

....

Your Tree's Roots

How much do you know about your family's past?

....

....

....

....

....

....

....

(There is space in the back of this book to fill out a family tree.
Or if you have one on your computer, consider printing it out
and tucking it into the pages of this book!)

"My grandmother Barbara's own favorite grandparent was her mother's, Lulu Dell Flickinger Robinson. Lulu went on a road trip in 1939 through North America with three women friends. Next to a story about J. Edgar Hoover in the *Indianapolis Star* was a headline about the trip: MEXICO LURES FOUR WIDOWED GRANDMOTHERS. My great-great-grandmother is quoted as saying, 'We believe life begins at sixty.'"

Name one distant ancestor you heard
about while growing up. Why were they
important to your family's history?

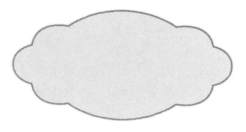

....

....

....

....

....

....

If you have one, get out your family's photo album.
What is your favorite photo in the album?

....

....

And what do you see when you look through photos
of your grandparents when they were young?

....

....

....

....

....

....

Were there any eccentric characters in your family tree?
What did they do?

Has anyone in your family served in the military?
List them below and describe their service.

....

....

....

....

....

....

....

....

....

Did anyone in your family ever save a life
or commit a heroic act? Describe them here.

What is one trait that you see running through
your family generation after generation?

....

....

....

....

....

....

....

....

"Given how little I cared for fishing, it surprised even me when, during high school and college summers in Maine, I started waking up early to go fishing with my father and grandfather. When you're a teenager, sleep is the most precious commodity. Yet there I was, rising before the sun was even up. I crept out of bed, slipped into my clothes, and tiptoed past my sleeping sister. I ran down the dewy grass path to the dock, where I met my dad and granddad by the water's edge.

Out there on the boat, in the morning chill, we talked about everything and nothing. Most of the hours we spent just looking out to sea, alone together."

Grandparents

Name your four grandparents:

How would you describe each of them?

MATERNAL

Grandmother   Grandfather

....

....

....

....

....

25

Grandmother

Grandfather

....

....

....

....

....

....

....

....

....

....

What did they do and what did their
approach to work teach you?

....

....

....

....

....

....

....

....

....

What memory do you have of time spent with one of them?

....

....

....

....

....

....

....

....

....

What was your closest grandparent's
favorite time of day?

....

Favorite holiday?

....

Favorite season?

....

Favorite hobby?

....

"People say, 'You remind

me so much of your mom!'

and I thank them. It is the

best compliment. In many

ways, I am like her: our

voices ring with the same

Texas twang; we have similar

cheekbones; we were both

teachers and love to read. But

in many ways, I am just trying

to keep up with her."

Parents

What is your mother's name and
how would you describe her?

What is your father's name and how would you describe him?

....

....

....

....

....

....

....

How did your parents meet?

....

....

....

....

....

....

....

....

How would you describe their relationship?

....

....

....

....

....

....

....

....

What work did your parents do?
What did their approach to work teach you?

What makes or made your parents happiest?

....

....

....

....

....

....

....

In what ways do you resemble your parents?

....

....

....

....

How are you different?

....

....

....

....

Did your parents have any special dreams for you?
Do you feel like they came true?

....

....

....

....

....

....

....

....

....

"Nothing makes me happier

than seeing my girls

whispering together. I think,

as I watch their precious

faces close together,

You don't yet know how

lucky you are that you have

each other. You will see

each other through love

and through pain.

And you will be by each

other's side, whatever comes."

Siblings

Name your siblings and their birth years.

Which sibling were you closest to
as a child and as an adult?

....

....

What is your favorite memory of
time spent with a sibling?

....

....

....

....

....

How has your relationship changed
with your siblings over the years?

....

....

....

....

....

....

Would you be close friends if you weren't related?

....

....

Write a letter to a sibling here.

"In Maine,

the oval table

is surrounded

by our throng

of aunts, uncles,

and raucous

cousins."

Aunts, Uncles, Cousins

Who are your closest aunts, uncles, and cousins?

What is a special time you spent with one of them?

....

....

....

....

....

What lesson did you learn from one of them?

....

....

....

....

Write a letter to an aunt, uncle, or cousin here.

"In a letter to my

daughters I wrote,

'It wasn't until

I held you—

with Grammee

by my hospital

bed—that I

really understood

my mom.'"

Children

Do you have children?
If so, list their names and birth years here.

....

....

....

....

....

....

....

....

Tell the story of a memorable birth experience.

How did you choose your children's names?
Are there any other names you seriously considered?

....

....

....

....

....

....

....

Have you had any moments as a parent that made you really understand your own parents?

....

....

....

....

....

....

What were your children's favorite toys? Draw one here.

Was there a favorite saying of any of the children in your family?

List any of your children's memorable "firsts" here.

....

....

First words.

....

....

....

....

....

....

First steps.

....

....

....

First day of school.

....

....

....

....

Write a letter to your children here.

"I turned over Ganny's

purse and thought of seeing

her hands pulling out a mint

to offer to a grandchild or

great-grandchild in church or

at a play in the hope that it

would keep them quiet.

One was never far away!"

Grandchildren

Do you have grandchildren?
If so, list their names and ages here.

Describe the first time you met one
of your grandchildren.

Write a letter to your grandchildren here.

PART II

Home and Away

"From his bedroom window those last few months of his life, Gampy looked out on the rocks where he'd scrambled as a young man and where, as a middle-aged man, he'd taught my father and my cousin Jebby to fly-fish. I know he thought of those happy times and wished he could feel the spray of the sea and the pull of his line once again."

Your Childhood Home

What place do you think of when you think of your childhood home?

....

....

....

....

....

....

What was your favorite room in that home and why?

Is the place still there? Who lives there now?

....

....

....

....

Draw a picture of it.

"In the wake of my Ganny's
and Gampy's deaths,
I confided in a friend that
sometimes I wished Henry
and I were more like my
grandparents.
I told her how I'd dreamed
that our home could be more
like theirs in Maine. Their love
created a glorious, nurturing
base for their children and
grandchildren. Entering that
house, you just felt joy.
*How can I emulate this in
my home?* I often thought."

Your Home Now

Describe where you live now.

....

....

....

....

....

....

....

....

Draw a floor plan and label it.

What is your favorite thing about your home?

"When people ask me

how I balance work

and small children,

I say, 'It's simple.

I don't.' I've been

blessed with

a lot of wonderful

things at once."

Work

What work do you do, both paid and unpaid?

....

....

....

....

....

....

....

....

Have you experienced any conflict between
your ambitions at work and home?
How have you found peace?

What does your work mean to you?

....

....

....

....

....

....

....

....

Who in your family encouraged you in your work and how?

....

....

....

....

....

....

....

....

If you didn't do the work you do,
what would you do instead?

....

....

....

....

....

....

....

....

"We dined with royalty, heads of states, authors, and activists. We even met the queen of England and managed to see the Texas Longhorns after they won the National Championship. We traveled with our parents to foreign lands and were deeply moved by what we saw. Trips to Africa inspired and motivated us to begin working for HIV/AIDS relief and for the rights of women and children all over the world."

Adventure

Are you by nature a world traveler or a homebody?

....

What parts of the world have you been to?

....

....

....

....

....

If you could go anywhere, where would it be?
Why?

Was anyone in your family especially intrepid?
Where did they go?

Did your family have vehicles that were important to them? Was there a family car that you remember fondly?

....

....

....

....

Draw a picture of it.

What was your family's favorite recreational activity (beach, ball game, picnic)?

What is the best family vacation you ever took?

Draw a picture of it.

PART III

Values

"At my paternal grandparents'
house in Maine, on the back of
every door my grandmother posted
a typed page of house rules.

Don't track in sand.

Hang up your towel.

Tell us if you'll be eating dinner out.

Make your bed.

With seventeen grandchildren
and eight great-grandchildren
running around, Ganny wanted to
make it clear what she expected
of us. These rules were simple,
practical guidelines for keeping
the house running smoothly,
but they also taught us respect.

House Rules

Did your grandparents have rules, either spoken or
implied? What were they, and did you follow them?

....

....

....

....

....

....

....

"Gampy had a list of guidelines for us, too. They were words of advice for living a life of passion and meaning, their humility and kindness as familiar as the loop in the cursive of his handwriting.

Don't get down when your life takes a bad turn.

Don't blame others for your setbacks.

When things go well, always give credit to others.

Don't talk all the time. Listen to your friends
and mentors and learn from them.

Don't brag about yourself. Let others point out
your virtues, your strong points.

Give someone a hand. When a friend is hurting,
show that friend you care.

Nobody likes an overbearing big shot.

As you succeed, be kind to people.
Thank those who help you along the way.

Don't be afraid to shed a tear when your heart
is broken or because a friend is hurting."

What practical rules do you have for your household?

What were your parents' rules for life?

What deeper rules do you try to follow to give
your family a life of purpose and meaning?

....

....

....

....

....

....

....

....

....

Is there a quote that inspires you?
Write it down here.

....

....

....

....

....

....

....

If your family had a family crest, what would be on it (perhaps a pencil if they valued education, or a sports team's logo if they were big fans)? Draw it here.

"Mila's preschool teacher, Maria, is one of the most incredible teachers I have ever encountered. She is a light of a human being—a tornado of hugs, smiles, and boundless energy, radiating warmth and goodness. In her tireless, tender way, she makes children feel safe, and she lets parents go off to work sure that their children will not only be taught the building blocks of math and reading but also be taught to love."

Education

What schools did you go to?

....

....

....

....

What schools did your parents go to?

....

....

....

What schools did your children go to?

....

....

....

....

How important was education when
you were growing up?

....

....

....

....

Is there a book with special meaning for your family?
What made it important to you?

....

....

....

....

....

....

....

....

Do any of your teachers stand
out as especially inspiring?

Write that teacher a letter here.

"Gazing at the rainbow,

I felt my heart fill with hope.

After the deepest pain, here

was an offering of peace.

There was no question in my

mind that God had put this

rainbow in the sky."

Faith

Were you raised within a religious tradition?

....

....

How does your understanding of spirituality differ
from your parents' or your children's?

....

....

....

....

....

Share a religious or secular prayer
for the future here.

Legacies

What messages did your parents get from their parents that were positive? Which ones were negative?

....

....

....

....

....

....

....

....

"As I lay in bed that night, I said a prayer to my grandmother Barbara. I told her, 'Thank you for seeing that all the women you love deserve to be free of the shame and distraction that might otherwise keep us from enjoying the blessings of this life.' I told her, too, that I hoped she was now able to hear a voice louder than her mother's and her stepmother's. I hoped that those fusty old calls to diet, to wear more makeup, or to try to look younger, slimmer, more alluring, were being drowned out by the strong, sure voices of her love-besotted husband, of her devoted children and grandchildren and friends."

What messages from your own childhood are you grateful for? Which have you rejected?

What messages do you hope to send to your own children about what is most important?

PART IV

Relationships

Marriage and Commitment

Why did you choose your spouse to commit to?

....

....

....

Tell your proposal story.

....

....

....

....

"At a recent talk I gave with my mom and sister at a women's panel in Dallas, my mom told the audience, 'Our son-in-law Henry is a saint. He's home with the kids while Jenna is here.' There is an unwelcome undertone to her portrayal of Henry as a saint. The corollary is that being married to me is akin to the martyrdom experienced by the saints. I have been to church. I know what some of those saints endured. Comparing marriage to me with the torments undergone by the holy stings a bit."

What was your wedding like?

....

....

....

....

....

....

Where was it and on what date?

....

....

What is the most beautiful wedding you've ever been to besides your own? What made it so special?

....

....

....

....

What is the greatest gift your spouse ever gave you?

....

....

....

....

Write a letter to your spouse here.

"We have had many cats over the years

Bernadette, also known as Bernie, who is nocturnal and meows wildly at night. When I was pregnant with Mila, I was so allergic to her because of my inability to take allergy medicine that she had to move in with my mother for my pregnancy. And then she didn't want to leave.

Sprity, the cat Barbara and I adopted when we were five and named after our favorite soft drink.

Baxter, the furry gray cat who ate dry macaroni and hid sponges under beds . . ."

Name some of the pets who have meant
the most to your family over the years.
What made them special?

....

....

....

....

....

....

....

....

Draw a picture of your favorite family pet.

"Surround yourself with

loyal friends. They'll protect

and calm you—and join in

on some of the fun."

Friends

Who were your best friends growing up?

....

....

....

What is your favorite memory of time spent
with a friend in your childhood?

....

....

....

....

Who are your best friends now?
Describe one of the best times you've
had with one of them.

....

....

....

....

....

....

....

Write a letter to your best friend thanking
them for their role in your life.

"On the subway to school,
Henry helped Mila send a text
to my mom that read:

We love you and your mom.
Is she okay? We want to
see her in July for her
100th birthday. Love, Mila

The text was decorated with
a birthday cake, a cat-face
emoji, a little girl, a baby,
and a detective."

Community

What do you do to help people around you—family members or strangers—who are suffering?

What causes are most important to you?

....

....

....

....

How do you find ways to give back?

....

....

....

List three wishes you have for the world.

1. ....

....

....

2. ....

....

....

3. ....

....

....

PART V

The Best and
Worst of Times

"Like my grandfather,

I'm very emotional.

Here are a times

I have cried:

- At kids' birthday parties,
  while watching my daughters
  dance with abandon.

- Walking down the aisle
  to marry Henry.

- At parent-teacher conferences,
  when I hear glowing reports.

- At all Kleenex commercials
  (*ironic, I know*)."

Laughter and Tears

List four times you have cried.

1. ....

....

2. ....

....

3. ....

....

4. ....

....

Fortunately,
I also laugh easily.

"As I read *Charlotte's Web* to my
little girls, one said to the other,
'It's okay. Spiders don't die.'

I had to break the news to
them that everything dies.

One then asked a question for which
I was unprepared: 'Even tacos?'

'No, honey!' I said. 'Tacos have
a big place in our home,
but they are not alive.'"

Who in your family can always make people laugh?
Write about a time they did something funny.

....

....

....

....

....

....

....

....

How does your family like to have fun?

Does your family have any great inside jokes?

"For four years, we spent our childhood holidays and vacations in the White House. We could almost feel the presence of all the great men and women who had lived here before us. When we played house, we sat behind the east sitting room's massive curtains as the light poured in illuminating her yellow walls. Our seven-year-old imaginations soared as we played in the enormous, beautiful rooms; our dreams, our games, as romantic as their surroundings. At night, the house sang us quiet songs through the chimneys as we fell asleep."

Celebrations

What is your favorite holiday and why?

....

....

....

....

....

....

....

What is one holiday tradition that you hope
continues in your family forever?

....

....

....

....

....

....

....

What is the best party your family ever threw
or attended? What made it so special?

....

....

....

....

....

....

....

....

Are there any songs that have special meaning
for your family? Write the lyrics here.

....

....

....

....

....

....

....

....

Who was the best cook in your family?

....

What was their signature dish?
Write or paste the recipe here.

"Henry knew his dad only in a wheelchair. John was diagnosed with polio at the age of thirty-four in 1973, five years before Henry was born, and he was paralyzed from the waist down from that point on. The way he acquired the disease was wildly unlikely, against million-to-one odds, like winning the worst lottery imaginable."

Tragedies

What struggles have you gotten
through together as a family?

....

....

....

....

What did you learn from the experience?

....

....

....

....

"Until it's your time to enter

the gates of heaven and join

those in your family who have

died, you walk to the gate and

then you walk back. You hope

that the sky is clear so you can

see the moon glowing over the

ocean, and you hope always

to walk with those you

love by your side."

Goodbyes

List the deaths that have affected you most.

....

....

....

....

....

....

....

....

What is the first family death you remember?

....

....

....

....

What do you believe happens after death?

....

....

....

....

Who has helped you cope with grief?

....

....

....

Were any friends especially helpful or
generous and what did they do?

....

....

What three things do you hope are
mentioned in your obituary?

1. ....

2. ....

3. ....

In what ways does your family honor the
memories of loved ones who are gone?

Write a eulogy or obituary for
someone you have lost.

PART VI

Milestones and Memories

My ancestors noted important dates in their family
Bible. Use this section to do the same. Milestones
might include births, deaths, marriages, graduations,
moves, or other major life events. Mementos might
include beloved letters or heirlooms. What treasures
(besides this journal!) do you hope are preserved and
handed down generation to generation?

Birthdays

January Birthdays

....

....

....

Febuary Birthdays

....

....

....

March Birthdays

....

....

....

April Birthdays

....

....

....

May Birthdays

....

....

....

June Birthdays

....

....

....

July Birthdays

....

....

....

August Birthdays

....

....

....

September Birthdays

....

....

....

October Birthdays

....

....

....

November Birthdays

....

....

....

December Birthdays

....

....

....

Important Events

Mementos

Draw your favorite mementos.

Our Family Tree

Create your own family tree! Cut out these shapes, or photocopy this page and cut them from the copy. Write the names of relatives on the shapes and paste or tape them on the tree.

Write a letter to someone who's
changed your life for the better.

....

....

....

....

....

....

....

....

Write a letter to someone who's changed your life for the better.

Write a letter to someone who's
changed your life for the better.

HarperCollins books may be purchased for educational, business, or sales promotional use. For information, please email the Special Markets Department at SPsales@harpercollins.com.

FIRST EDITION

Designed by Bonni Leon-Berman

Illustrations by Oana Befort

Library of Congress Cataloging-in-Publication Data has been applied for.

ISBN 978-0-06-305139-3

21 22 23 24 25   LSC   10 9 8 7 6 5 4 3 2 1